BEARS OF THE WORLD™

BROWN BEARS

DIANA STAR HELMER

The Rosen Publishing Group's
PowerKids Press™
New York

Many thanks to Don Middleton, member of the International Bear Research and Management Association, International Wildlife Rehabilitation Council, and founder and webmaster of The Bear Den, at http://www.nature-net.com/bears/

Published in 1997 by The Rosen Publishing Group, Inc.
29 East 21st Street, New York, NY 10010

First Edition

Book Design: Danielle Primiceri

Photo Credits: Cover shots © Mark Newman/International Stock, © PhotoDisc; pp. 4, 12, 15, 19, 20 © Mark Newman/International Stock; p. 7 © Scott Wm. Hanrahan/International Stock; p. 8 © Will Regan/International Stock; p. 11 © Joseph Van Os/Image Bank; p. 16 © Ron Sanford/International Stock.

Helmer, Diana Star, 1962–
    Brown bears / Diana Star Helmer.
        p.   cm. — (Bears of the world)
    Includes index.
    Summary: Examines the physical characteristics, behavior, and habitats of the brown bear.
    ISBN 0-8239-5131-6
    1. Brown bear—Juvenile literature. [1. Brown bear. 2. Bears.] I. Title. II. Series: Helmer, Diana Star, 1962– Bears of the world.
    QL737.C27H4442 1997
    599.784—dc21   96-1933
                                                                                                      CIP
                                                                                                      AC

Manufactured in the United States of America

Table of Contents

Brown Bears Around the World

Brown bears live in more countries than any other kind of bear. Brown bears used to live in much of the western United States. The state of California even has a picture of one kind of brown bear, called a grizzly, on its flag. But no grizzlies have lived in California for many years. In North America, brown bears now live mostly in the far north, in western Canada and Alaska.

Brown bears live near mountains, rivers, and **meadows** (MEH-dohz). They live in Spain, France, Italy, Norway, Sweden, Finland, and Russia. Brown bears also live on the Japanese island of Hokkaido.

◀ *Brown bears live all over the world.*

Don't Judge a Bear By Its Color

Brown bears come in many different sizes and colors. Some brown bears are small. They weigh only about 300 pounds! Other brown bears, such as the **Kodiak** (KOH-dee-ak) bear, can weigh up to 1,500 pounds. Kodiak bears live near the Pacific Ocean in Alaska.

Not all brown bears are brown. Some are the color of toast. Some have blond fur or red fur. Some brown bears are even black. If you can't tell a brown bear by its color, how can you tell?

Brown bear fur comes in many colors—even blond! ▶

So How Do You Know?

Brown bears are curvy, from their noses to their rumps. A brown bear's forehead reaches up high from its nose. Its shoulders make one curve, and its bear bottom another. Brown bears have long, shaggy fur.

Brown bears also have long claws to dig up food. Their claws are often too big to climb trees. So, if you see a brown-colored bear in a tree, it's probably not a brown bear.

Climbing isn't impossible for brown bears. But it isn't easy either. That's why brown bears often live in open places, such as meadows and river valleys.

◄ *A brown bear's long claws make it hard to climb trees.*

Bear Space

No matter where bears live, each bear has its own **territory** (TEHR-ih-TOH-ree). A bear's territory is like a person's town. A bear will share parts of its territory. Bears share forest trails the way people share sidewalks. Bears eat at the same places—but they don't often eat together. Bears like to be alone.

In bear territories, each bear keeps its own special space. Each bear scratches marks on the trees around its territory to tell other bears to stay away.

Brown bears scratch marks into the trees around their ▶ territory. This tells other bears that this is their area.

Big Food, Big Bears

Brown bears are **omnivores** (AHM-nih-vohrz). They eat almost anything! Bears eat mice, roots, berries, nuts, grass, and bugs. Brown bears even keep nature clean by eating dead or sick animals. Eating meat and fish makes bears grow big. But most of the meals that brown bears eat are made up of plants.

In the fall, brown bears eat almost all day and night. Their fur grows thick and warm. A brown bear might eat enough food during the fall to gain six pounds of fat every day. This extra fat feeds a bear's body while the bear **hibernates** (HY-ber-nayts), or sleeps, all winter.

◀ *Eating fish or meat helps a bear grow bigger.*

Bear Families

When a female brown bear is five years old, she is ready to **mate** (MAYT). Brown bears mate during the summer. After a male and female mate, babies may start growing in the female's body. While the mother's body gains fat to hibernate, the unborn cubs won't grow much. They cannot grow until their mother has enough body fat for her long winter sleep.

Brown bear cubs are born in the late winter, after ▶
their mother wakes up from her winter nap.

Den Mothers

As winter begins, each bear finds a den in which to hibernate. Dens can be made out of logs, caves, or holes in the ground. Hibernating bears breathe slowly. Their hearts beat slower, too.

The unborn babies in a **pregnant** (PREG-nunt) female bear grow while she hibernates. The cubs, which are often twins, are born in January or February. They drink milk, sleep, and grow until spring.

Bears come out of hibernation in April or May. Mother bears that weighed 500 pounds in the fall may weigh only 300 pounds in the spring.

◀ *Mother bears and their cubs are the last brown bears to come out of hibernation in the spring.*

Keeping Cubs Safe

Cubs leaving the den are the size of puppies. They are in danger once they leave. Male brown bears don't know which cubs are theirs, and they don't care. They hunt many small animals, including cubs. Wolves, lions, and eagles also hunt bear cubs.

Brown bear mothers try to keep their cubs safe. They teach their cubs what to eat, and where to find food. By fall, cubs no longer drink their mother's milk. They eat and get ready to hibernate. Cubs hibernate with their mother for two winters. Then they go off to live on their own, and the females mate again.

Mother bears stay close to their cubs until the cubs are old enough to find food and stay safe. ▶

Safety with Bears

Bears like to be alone. If bears hear people, they stay away. So when you are in the woods where bears live, go with friends. Talk as you walk.

Surprised bears may attack, especially mother bears. If you see a brown bear, don't look in its eyes. Back away slowly. If a brown bear touches you, roll into a ball. Don't move. It may go away.

Bears sometimes come near people when they smell food. Stay away from bear food, like berries and dead animals. Keep all human food and garbage in **airtight** (AYR-tyt) containers away from where you will be sleeping.

◄ *Brown bears are beautiful animals, but they are very dangerous. Stay away from any bears you see in the woods, no matter how friendly they may look.*

A Small Planet

Long ago, the world had more bears and fewer people. Today, there are more people. People need more land on which to live. They take the wood from forests to build their houses. When cities grow, bears have less space in which to live.

It is important to keep some areas wild. Wild plants in these places clean the air. Plants such as trees help the earth stay cooler in the summer and warmer in the winter. Small wild animals spread and plant seeds. Bears make sure that small animals, like mice and squirrels, don't eat all the seeds and plants.

Earth needs bears' help to **survive** (ser-VYV). And bears need our help to survive on Earth.

Glossary

airtight (AYR-tyt) A container that keeps the air out and the smells in.

hibernate (HY-ber-nayt) To sleep through the winter without eating.

Kodiak (KOH-dee-ak) An island near Alaska where large brown bears live.

mate (MAYT) A special joining of the male and female bodies. After mating, the female may become pregnant.

meadow (MEH-doh) A small, flat area of land with grasses and plants.

omnivore (AHM-nih-vohr) An animal that eats both plants and other animals.

pregnant (PREG-nunt) When a female animal has an unborn baby inside her body.

survive (ser-VYV) To keep living.

territory (TEHR-ih-TOH-ree) A space that an animal or group of animals takes as its own.

Index